EVERYTHING I KNOW about PIRATES

Everything I Know about PIRATES

A collection of made-up facts, educated guesses, and silly pictures about bad guys of the high seas.

WRITTEN & ILLUSTRATED by TOM LICHTENHELD

SCHOLASTIC INC.
New York Toronto London Auckland Sydney
Mexico City New Delhi Hong Kong

I don't know much about pirates, but I know enough to draw some pictures. And I can make up enough to draw some more pictures.

The most important thing about pirates, as I remember, is that they're mean. Everything about them comes from meanness. Their looks, their manners (or lack thereof), their boats, and even their language.

First, let's look at a pirate's wardrobe. On their feet, pirates always wear boots. Because pirates are thieves, their boots are usually stolen, which means the boots are too big. That's why they have to fold their boots at the top, so the boots won't cover the bottom edges of their pants, which are really cool.

VENTILATED
to PREVENT
TOE CRUD

Fig. 1

P irate pants are always black but can be made of any material available. Cotton is a classic, wool drapes nicely, but the practical pirate chooses a fast-drying nylon. Notice the shark-bite hems. Most pirates have "walked the plank" at least once, and that's how their pants get this snazzy pattern along the bottom.

SHIPNECK ~ LIKE A LARGE BOAT NECK

b.o.

WHY PIRATES MAKE LOUSY BRAIN SURGEONS

P irate shirts are usually striped. They're probably stolen from the British navy, or maybe they're old prison uniforms. Anyway, the horizontal stripes make the pirates look wider and bigger and meaner than they really are.

PIRATES MEND THEIR OWN SWORD STAB HOLES.

SECRET PIRATE KNOTS

LONG JOHN'S BELT KNOT

SQUARE-PEG KNOT

NOT-SO-GOOD KNOT

Also notice that most pirates use rope for a belt, and that they have their own secret rope-belt knots, revealed in this top-secret pirate diagram.

PIRATES spend Sunday afternoons reading the color comics.

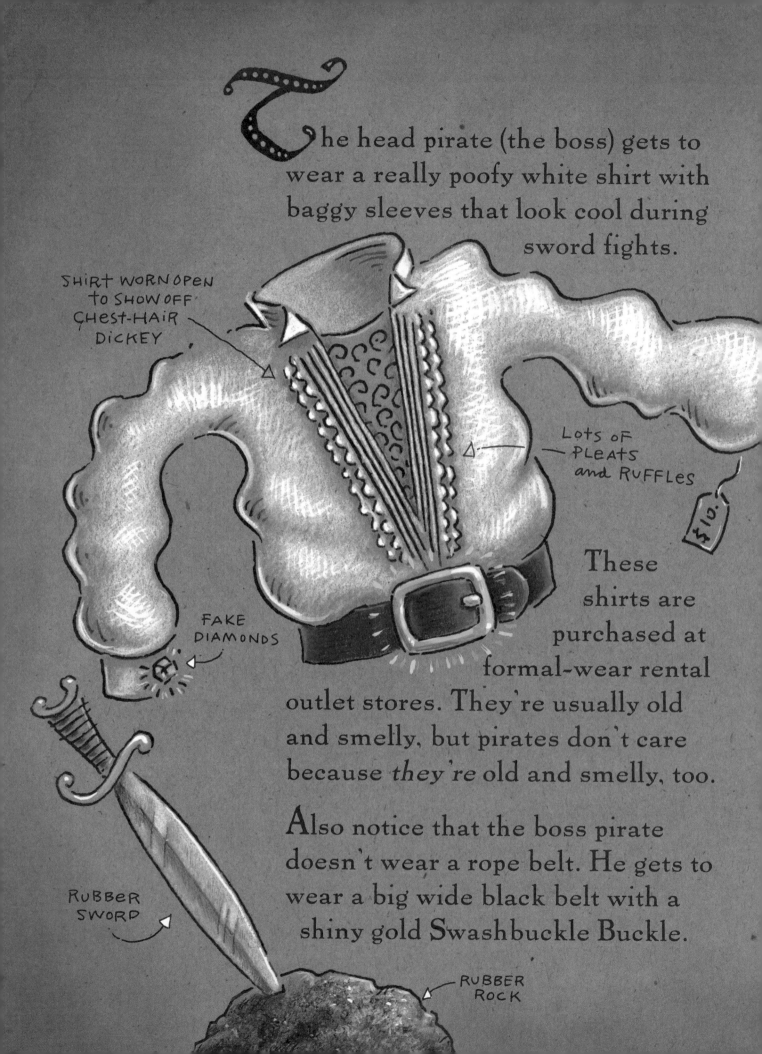

The head pirate (the boss) gets to wear a really poofy white shirt with baggy sleeves that look cool during sword fights.

SHIRT WORN OPEN TO SHOW OFF CHEST-HAIR DICKEY

LOTS OF PLEATS and RUFFLES

$10.

FAKE DIAMONDS

These shirts are purchased at formal-wear rental outlet stores. They're usually old and smelly, but pirates don't care because *they're* old and smelly, too.

Also notice that the boss pirate doesn't wear a rope belt. He gets to wear a big wide black belt with a shiny gold Swashbuckle Buckle.

RUBBER SWORD

RUBBER ROCK

A pirate with scaredy-pants

If a pirate embarrasses his pirate buddies by losing his courage in the heat of battle, they'll sneak into his room at night and sew the legs of his pants together. That way, the easily frightened pirate can't run away in the middle of a sword fight. This is where the term "scaredy-pants" actually comes from.

Pirates often wear polka-dot hankies. The polka dots are actually old booger stains.

Pirates like to wear hats, but they're not too fussy about them. They are, however, quite particular about their eye patches.

PIRATE HEADGEAR

The "KING'S HAT"
Worn sideways just to BUG the ROYAL Family

STANDARD ISSUE PIRATE HAT

PITTSBURGH Pirate Hat

Pirates often get their eyes poked out when they "walk the plank" and a clumsy old swordfish pokes them in the eye. In fact, pirates have lots of mishaps. Which is why they sport hooks in place of hands and wooden poles in place of legs.

The "FITS-'EM-ALL" EYE PATCH

WITH ELASTO-STRAP

The way a pirate loses his leg is when he goes swimming in the ocean and he puts his toe in the water to see if it's cold and a big shark comes along and *bites his leg off!*

Pirates with lots of peg legs and eye patches and hooks are the scariest kind, but that doesn't make much sense because it really just means they're clumsy guys and not necessarily mean. Go figure!

OOPS

HEY! WATCH IT, BUB!

WHY PIRATES ALWAYS NEED EYE PATCHES.

irates go in for fashion accessories that make a visual statement, which is good because their verbal communication consists largely of belches and grunts. They like to wear shiny earrings, mean-looking tattoos, and oversized pinkie rings.

pirAte Tattoo and pinkie Ring

Of course, any pirate worth his sea salt has to have a nasty old parrot perched on his shoulder. And they're not named Polly, either. They have big, hairy names like Butch or Spike.

Pirates are also careful to stay good and stinky. They eat lots of garlic and never take baths. If a pirate gets caught in the rain and gets accidentally clean, he'll go down to the poop deck and sit in a pile of fish guts until he works up a good, nostril-burning stink. Pirates are also fussy about their hair. The desired look is kind of matted and crusty, like one of my cats' puked-up hair balls.

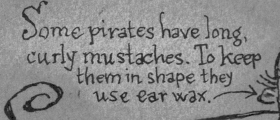

Some pirates have long, curly mustaches. To keep them in shape they use ear wax.

When pirates finally get their outfits and hairdos worked out, they get busy attacking other people's ships and stealing their stuff.

Sometimes it takes more than body odor, missing limbs, and tattered, old clothes to frighten people completely off their ships. In these cases, pirates will use weapons.

Their favorite weapon is the trusty old sword because it's maintenance-free, lightweight, and versatile in battle (It slices! It dices! It makes french fries out of French sailors!).

Pirates also like cannons because they're loud and smelly, and on those rare occasions when they're aimed accurately, there's nothing like a cannonball for putting a big ol' hole in somebody else's ship. When not being used in battle, cannons make great paperweights to keep the secret treasure maps from flying all over.

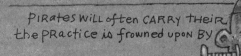

PiRATes WILL often CARRY THEIR KNIVES In their MOUTHS, ALTHOUGH the PRACTICE is frowned upoN BY the AMERICAN DENTAL ASSOCIATION.

Here's the most important thing . . . the pirate ship. Pirates don't actually build their own ships because they're so clumsy that they're afraid to use power tools. Besides, they're too lazy to do that much work.

So they go to nautical history museums and steal the ships while the museum guards are busy shushing groups of rowdy school-children. Then they put the skull and crossbones all over the sails and throw rotten garbage around until it starts to feel like home.

Pirate ships are designed for maximum chaos during battle. That's why pirates keep lots of loose cannons and cannonballs onboard,

CROW'S NEST

Wind

DENTAL FLOSS STORAGE

JUNGLE GYM

THE UPDECK

BACK

I SMELL PIRATES.

Just IN CASE

GLASS BOTTOM (OPTIONAL)

which roll around willy-nilly in the heat of battle. They also use lots of gunpowder because it smells like rotten eggs (yum!).

Meanwhile, some of the pirates are climbing up the jungle gyms like one-eyed monkeys and yelling nasty, mean stuff like, "Avast, ye vermin!" and, "Swab the deck yourself, Larry!"

Eventually, all the pirates get bored with the fighting and get together over a root beer and tell lies about how mean they were in the battle.

WHITE SALE

BIG SALE

WHAT A BIG WORD!

JIB

the POKER

MAST

PEG LEG STORAGE

BOWL-O-RAMA

FRONT

UP

W E

CUTAWAY VIEW

I SMELL PIRATES, TOO.

NMOD

BISCUITS & ROOT BEER

CARGO

BARNACLES

Here's the deal with "the plank." If a pirate was really, *really* bad, like if he spilled pancake syrup all over the secret treasure map, he'd have to "walk the plank" as punishment.

A really sturdy plank is made out of solid oak and mounted to the ship with one-quarter-inch brass lag bolts and then coated with a marine-grade varnish. But one of those old boards that your dad has piled up behind the garage would probably work just fine.

SHIP'S ART COLLECTION

Sometimes, when there weren't too many hungry sharks around, pirates would use the plank to practice their fancy diving tricks (they invented the "cannonball"), but this has become a rarity due to the high cost of liability insurance. In a tragic loss to the world of sports, pirates haven't had an Olympic diving team since the late 1700s.

I WANT TO RIP YOUR PANTS.

DEAD PIRATE

The HISTORY of THE SKULL AND CROSSBONES

History is a funny thing. (Actually, it's not, otherwise you'd be reading a history book instead of this one.) For many years, it was believed that the skull and crossbones was first discovered by pirates on the inside of a desk in a seventh-grade classroom in De Kalb, Illinois. However,

Seventh-grade class desk
DE KALB, ILLINOIS

since scientists have discovered that dinosaurs actually evolved from birds, they now figure that the skull and crossbones must have come from somewhere weird, too.

The new theory is that the skull and crossbones was the result of years of trial and error.

1620
HOT DOG and CROSSBONES
Problems: ① Mustard drips.
② Not very scary.

1685
CIRCUS CLOWN and CROSSBONES
Problems: ① Hard to paint on flag. ② Too scary.

Shown below are the ideas that pirates tried over the years. They wanted a flag that would warn people on other ships that some low-down scoundrels were about to attack them, sink their ship, and take all their shiny things.

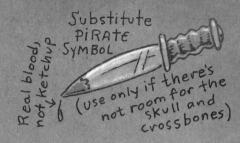

Real blood, not ketchup

Substitute PIRATE SYMBOL

(use only if there's not room for the skull and crossbones)

The final design, as this theory goes, was invented by Leonardo "Peg Leg" da Vinci, who also invented air and the Jacuzzi tub.

Regardless of where the skull and crossbones came from, pirates are so crazy about the darn thing that they put it all over their stuff – their sails, their hats, probably even on their underwear when they go to pirate camp, so it doesn't get mixed up in the laundry.

1716
HOUSE and CROSSBONES
Problems: ① Made pirates homesick.
② Houses not invented yet.

1792
SKULL and CROSSBONES
Way to go, Leonardo!

The purpose of a pirate's life, besides meanness, is to hunt for buried treasure because it's a lot easier than robbing from other ships and you get to carry around really cool maps called "secret treasure maps." These maps were printed on waterproof paper made to look like crusty old parchment.

Sometimes a pirate would refuse to use a map at all and just wander aimlessly around the ocean, refusing to even stop to ask directions. These were usually Dad pirates.

Some secret treasure maps were so big that the pirates would have to roll them up and put them way up high out of reach, like these guys are doing in this rare and valuable pirate photo.

the ONLY thingS CRABBieR than PiRAtES are CRABS!

When the pirates followed the map successfully, they would find a huge black "X" painted on the ground. This always marked the spot for buried treasure (except for that one time when it turned out to be a priceless piece of modern art).

Chocolate coins were more valuable than real gold.

Then they'd dig up a big old steamer trunk chock-full of gold coins, jewelry, and high-end Japanese electronics, although they would settle for anything shiny. Then they would split the "booty" – that's pirate talk for stolen goods – among the crew.

They'd be pretty pooped out after all this map-reading, hole-digging, and booty-splitting, so they'd sit down and celebrate over a glass of punch. Pirates like punch because they get to say to each other, "Hey, how about a little punch?!" Then they haul off and punch each other.

The next day the pirates would get up and draw a new, even cooler secret treasure map.

A QUIZ: Which kind of DOG would a PIRATE have?

IF YOU DID NOT PICK C, YOU MUST START OVER FROM PAGE ONE!

A   B   C

The Howard Pyle pose

It's important that pirates look mean and cool at all times, otherwise they can be mistaken for just surly, badly dressed sailors.

So, when they're not too busy stealing other people's clothing, getting their legs bitten off, or doing cannonball dives, pirates practice their jaunty pirate poses. Plus, they have a special way of smiling so their true meanness still shows through. It's called the Pirate Sneer, and it looks like this. >>>> (Try it on your parents.)

PIRATES DON'T WALK~ THEY SWAGGER.

HAT WORN AT A RAKISH ANGLE

ARM LEANING ON A PILE OF SEAGULL POOP

the "DEVIL-MAY-CARE" pose

PIRATES DON'T SHAVE OFTEN.

What about food? Pirates gotta eat, too!! Since there aren't many McDonald's restaurants on the high seas, pirates have to use their wits to rustle up some grub. Pirates eat a lot of cafeteria food, which they swipe from fish schools. When they're feeling especially mean and hungry, they like to eat fish fingers.

FISH SCHOOL CAFETERIA LADY

tee hee!

If all else fails, pirates will eat the food they brought onboard, which is usually dried biscuits that get infested with weevils and maggots. They eat the weevils and maggots, then use the rock-hard biscuits to play their favorite game, called "Conk the Captain."

Most pirate voyages include complimentary peanuts and beverages. Besides punch, they offer rum, which pirates like to sing about at Christmastime: "Ho-ho-ho and a bottle of rum!"

"CONK the CAPTAIN"

PiRates Like PARRots, but they're Not so FOND of SEAGULLS.

PIRATE

NAME CHART

pick one word from each column.

LONG	JOHN	KIDD
BLACK	EYE	BART
EVIL	BEARD	BONNY*
HOOK	LEG	JACK
CAPTAIN	CALICO	BOB
PEG	SKULL	NED
BIG	BANDIT	SAM
STUB	BOOT	BRUCE
BLIND	TOOTH	WILLY
ONE	PATCH	TOM**
BLUE	LIPS	HENRY
LIMP	WRECK	JOE

* WARNING! THIS IS A GIRL PIRATE NAME.

** OKAY, NOT A GOOD PIRATE NAME, BUT I HAD TO PUT IT IN THE CHART.

Now, if all this pirate stuff sounds good to you, the first thing you're going to need is a decent, nasty pirate name. Use this handy chart to create one for yourself. Any combination is guaranteed to be an authentic mean pirate name.

It's important to have your very own pirate name by the time you go to the annual pirate convention, because they're not going to let you in with a name like Nathan or Ashley.

Yo!

sup!.

pirates ARE friendly At tHeir ANNUAL CONVENTION.

HELLO MY NAME IS EVIL SKULL NED

It's also important that you know how to talk like a pirate, so I've included a list of pirate words on the next page. Once you memorize a few pirate words, get yourself a pirate name, and perfect the Pirate Sneer, you'll be ready to shove off into the nasty world of piratedom.

That's it! Everything I know about pirates! (If you think I've forgotten anything, feel free to make it up for yourself!)

Official PIRATE GLOSSARY

[Words to use when you want to sound like a real pirate!]

Aaarrgh! A universal pirate expletive. Best when used in conjunction with the Pirate Sneer.

Ahoy 1. Hello. 2. Howdy. 3. Good Day. 4. Yo! S'up?

Avast! 1. "Hey you, cut that out!" 2. A lot of space.

Booty (2.)

Booty 1. A batch of stolen goods; jewels, gold coins, Swiss watches. 2. Cute little bedroom slipper.

Bow 1. The front end of a pirate ship, up by the poker. 2. What pirates do after giving a good performance on talent night.

Buccaneer 1. A fancy French word for "pirate." 2. How much a pirate pays to get his ears pierced.

Crow's Nest 1. A platform up at the top of the mast where pirates go to play "Conk the Captain." 2. A nest that crows live in, you silly.

EARS PIERCED: $1⁰⁰

Davy Jones's Locker 1. The bottom of the ocean, home of dead pirates and crabby crabs. 2. A little-known shrine at Lincoln Junior High School, frequented by aging fans of the Monkees.

Doubloon 1. A Spanish gold coin, treasured by pirates. 2. Two balloons tied together.

Galleon 1. A large Spanish ship. When loaded with gold coins, valuable jewels and luxury cars, it was a cargo ship. When loaded with cannons, it was a battleship. 2. Four quarts.

KISS THE COOK

Galley The kitchen on a ship, usually long and skinny (unlike the cook who occupies it).

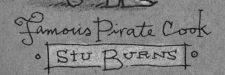

Famous Pirate Cook
Stu Burns

Head 1. The bathroom on a ship. 2. What a pirate stands to lose if he's not good at sword-fighting.

Jolly Roger 1. Another word for the skull and crossbones. 2. The name of the good-natured guy who modeled for the skull and crossbones.

Jolly Roger (1.)

Marooned 1. To be left alone on a desert island. A form of punishment used on pirates who didn't clean their rooms. 2. To be colored purple.

Mutiny A revolt by the crew, overthrowing the captain of the ship. On pirate ships, this would usually happen because somebody on the crew wanted the captain's poofy shirt.

Jolly Roger (2.)

Pieces of Eight 1. Spanish silver dollars, often a major portion of the "booty." 2. (slang) Pirate throw-up.

Poop Deck 1. Stop giggling. 2. It's not what you think.

Port 1. One side of the ship, I can never remember which. 2. The sound a nickel makes when you drop it into the toilet.

yawn

Starboard 1. The other side of the ship. 2. What happens to actors when they're not making a pirate movie.

Stern 1. The back end of the ship, opposite the poker end. 2. The kind of look you'll get from your parents when you give them the Pirate Sneer.

Davy Jones's Locker (1.)

ISBN 0-439-28571-2

12 11 10 9 8 7 6 5 4 3   6 7 8/0

Printed in the U.S.A.   40

First Scholastic printing, April 2001

Book design by Tom Lichtenheld

The text for this book is set in Pabst.

The illustrations are rendered in ink, colored pencil, gouache, pastels, and ear wax.

To JAN MILLER for her endless support and ADAM LICHTENHELD for his inspiration.